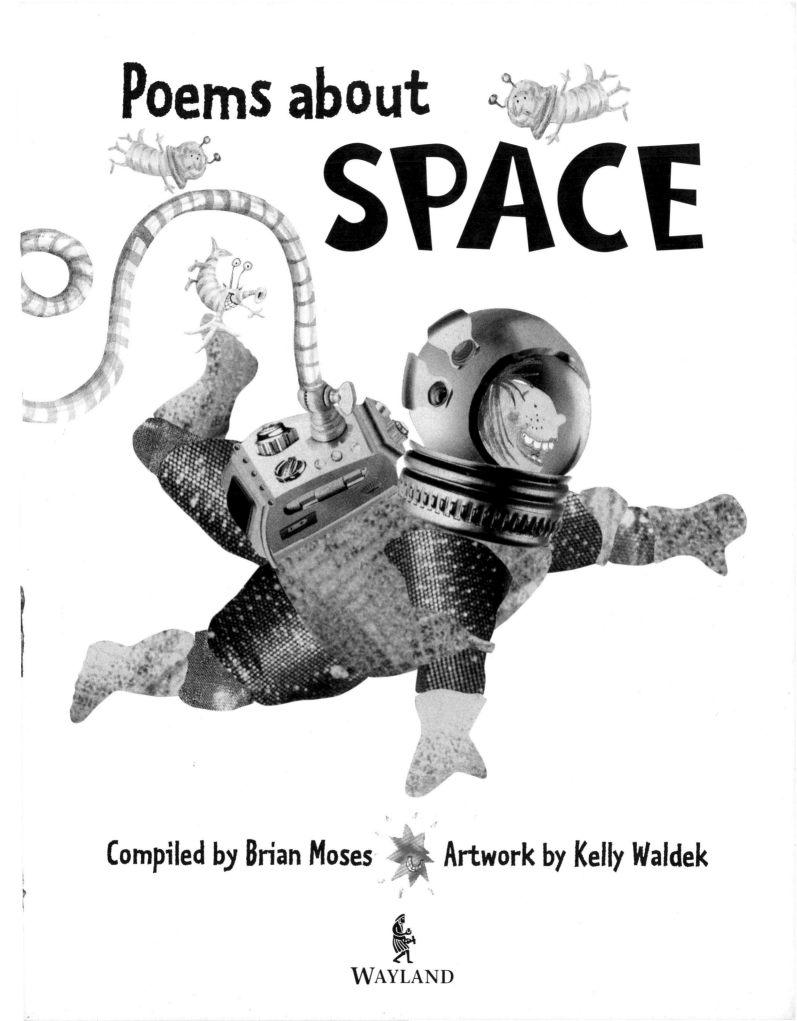

Poems about
SPACE

Compiled by Brian Moses   Artwork by Kelly Waldek

WAYLAND

Titles in the series:

Poems about Animals
Poems about Food
Poems about School

Editor: Sarah Doughty
Designer: Tessa Barwick

find Wayland on the Internet at http://www.wayland.co.uk

First published in 1999 by
Wayland Publishers Ltd
61 Western Road, Hove
East Sussex, BN3 1JD

© Copyright 1999 Wayland Publishers Ltd

British Library Cataloguing in Publication Data
Poems about Space – (Wayland poetry collections)
    1. Outer space – Juvenile poetry 2. Children's poetry,
English
    I. Moses, Brian, 1950 –
821.9'14'08'0356

ISBN 0 7502 2436 3

Printed and bound by Edições ASA, Portugal

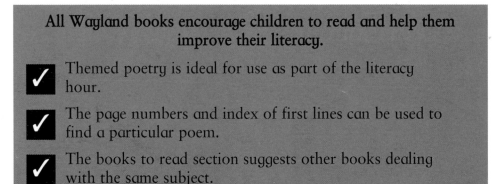

**All Wayland books encourage children to read and help them
improve their literacy.**

✓ Themed poetry is ideal for use as part of the literacy
hour.

✓ The page numbers and index of first lines can be used to
find a particular poem.

✓ The books to read section suggests other books dealing
with the same subject.

Contents

Rocket

I am a rocket
crouched on the ground,
waiting quietly
without a sound.

Light this fuse
on my little toe. . .
Ready for take-off?
Here I go:

Tony Mitton

WHOOSH!

Rocket Rhyme

10, 9, 8, 7, 6, 5, 4

here is a rocket
ready to roar.

3, 2, 1

blast off to the sky.
There goes the rocket.
Wave bye-bye.

Tony Mitton

Our Spaceship

Make me a spaceship Dad,
one that will really fly.
Make me a spaceship Dad,
let's take off into the sky.

Let's take a trip to the moon,
let's play games on Mars,
let's take off once again
and visit all the stars.

Make me a spaceship Dad,
one that will really fly.
We'll have such fun in space
just you and I.

Brian Moses

WHAT'S THAT SHAPE?

A shoe?
A shell?
A shark?
A sheep?
A slimy slug?
A sloth asleep?
A shadow's smile?
A skull? A ski?

A ship that sails the solar seas?
A ship that sails the solar sea?
? ? ? ? ?

*Gina
Douthwaite*

Rocket Horse

"I've got a rocket horse," said Jilly.
Her friends all laughed, "Don't be silly.
It's a rocking horse, like any other."
But Jilly just smiled and so did her brother.

Their rocket horse took them anywhere,
above the clouds and through the air.
They took a trip to Disneyland
where rocket horse marched behind the band.

Then off they zoomed far into space,
past the Moon with a smile on his face.
On they flew to the planet Mars
with rocket horse jumping from star to star.

"I'm hungry," said Jilly
"it's time to go."
So they rode very fast
down a rainbow. . .

. . . all the way home.

Brian Moses

9

The Moon

The moon is just a big potato floating in the sky
And little men from outer space are often passing by.
If they're feeling hungry they just eat a bit for dinner,
That's why the moon is sometimes fat,
but other times it's thinner.

Kjartan Poskitt

The Moon

The moon is a banana shape
That hangs
Up in the sky.
And when the sun
Has turned away.
The moon is there
To take its place.
To shine down on the earth
With a smiling face.
Its moonbeams are a slide
Where the fairies play.

Jamie Booth (aged 6)

Is the Moon tired?

Is the moon tired? She looks so pale
    Within her misty veil;
She scales the sky from east to west,
    And takes no rest.

Before the coming of the night
    The moon shows papery white;
Before the dawning of the day
    She fades away.

Christina Rosetti

Moonlight

I saw moonlight lying on the ground,
I stooped and touched the ground
   with my hand.
And found it was common earth,
Dust was in my palm.

P.J. Chaudhury (India)

Only the Moon

When I was young I thought
The new moon was a cradle
The full moon was granny's round face.

The new moon was a banana
The full moon was a big cake.

When I was a child
I never saw the moon
I only saw what I wanted to see.

And now I see the moon
It's the moon
Only the moon, and nothing but the moon.

Wong May (Singapore)

14

Footprints on the Moon

There were men on the moon once.
They travelled through space
and found that the moon
was a dry, dusty place.

They collected some moon rocks
and had a look round
and left lots of footprints
there on the ground.

They couldn't stay long
as the moon has no air,
but the foot prints they left
in the dust are still there.

Marian Swinger

Star Travelling

I'm a twinkling eye
I'm a dancing light,
I'm a tiny snowdrop
I'm a splash of white.

I'm a dash of silver
I'm a jewel too far,
I'm a wish still waiting
I'm a shooting star.

Andrew Collett

Star Wish

Starlight. Starbright.
First star I see tonight.
I wish I may, I wish I might
Have the wish I wish tonight

Traditional

Riddle

I may look flat
But I'm round as a ball,
I feel quite still
But I'm not still at all,
I travel constantly
Spinning as I go,
From space I'm swirly
With a blue pearly glow.
What am I?

Sue Cowling

Answer: Earth

HELP, HELP!
Walk for your lives!

Astronomers have spotted
the first green trace
of slime in space.

It comes from a planet
Ten million miles away
Space slugs, the experts say.

It is an invasion
But we on Earth have no need to fear
The slug's top speed is one mile a year.

John Coldwell

21

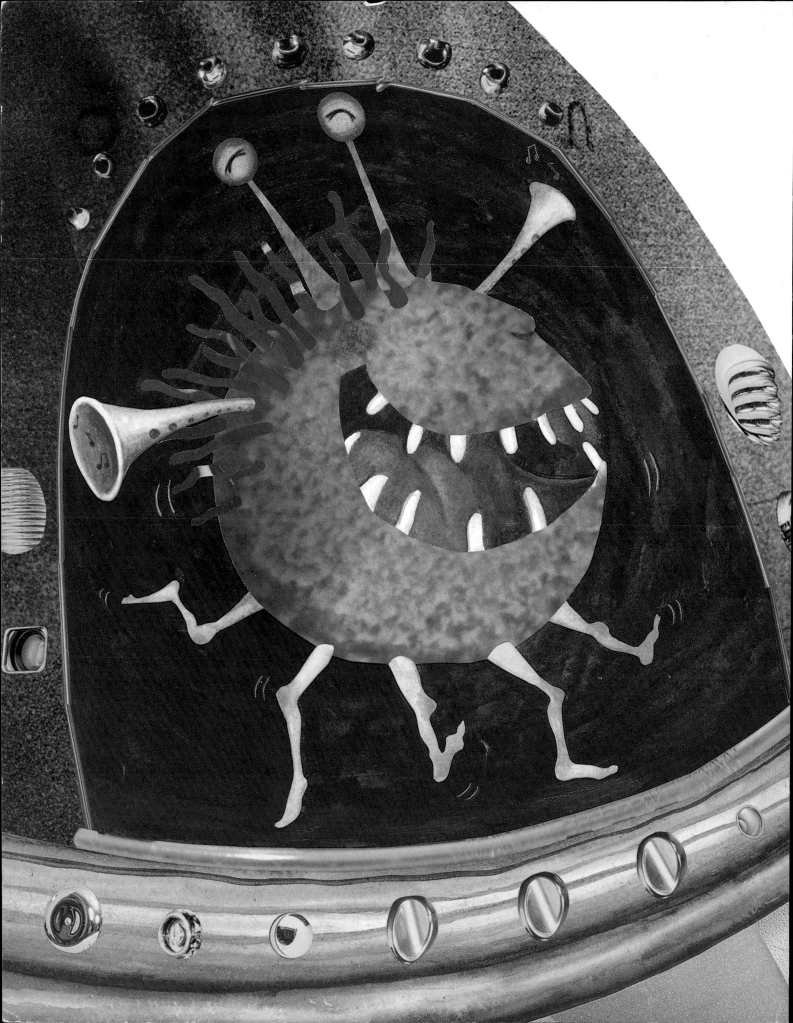

The Alien

The alien
Was as round as the moon.
Five legs he had
And his ears played a tune.
His hair was pink
And his knees were green,
He was the funniest thing I'd seen.
As he danced in the door
Of his strange spacecraft.
He looked at me –
And laughed and laughed!

Julie Holder

Brief Encounter

Zooming on and on
Through space,
I want to see
A Martian's face,
And when I've said,
"Hallo", well then
I want to zoom
Back home again.

Clive Webster

Three Cheers

I think we've been spotted from Venus;
A big bug-eyed monster has seen us.
    It's fierce and it's red
      With great horns on its head.
Three cheers for the distance between us!

Barry Buckingham

The Visitor

From beyond
the Solar System,
from deep
in Outer Space,
a visitor with
a long, bright tail
came to show
its fiery face!

Racing towards
our planet,
faster than
a rocket ship,
the comet zoomed
then turned around
to start its
return trip.

Following
its orbit,
going back
from where it came,
but a hundred years
or so from now
it'll visit
us again!

Tony Langham

The Solar System

Magical Mercury zooms
    through the night,
Venomous Venus is
    misty and bright.

Earth is the place where
    we curl up in bed,
Mars is a planet
    that's dusty and red.

Jupiter still has a spot
    on its face,
Saturn wears rings as
    it sparkles in Space.

Uranus floats like a
    gassy balloon,
Neptune's as blue as a
    dreamy lagoon.

Pluto is tiny and turns
    far away –
That's all the planets.
      There's no more to say.

Clare Bevan

Further Information

Following on from any reading of a poem, either individually or in groups, check with the children that they have understood what the poem is about. Ask them to point out any difficult words or lines and explain these. Ask children how they feel about the poem. Do they like it? Is there a particular section or line in the poem that they really enjoy?

Children may wish to learn one of the poems or to add actions. Tony Mitton's poems are both 'action rhymes' and children may like to suggest what sort of actions would fit the verses. Once the ideas have been agreed, the poem and actions can be practised and then performed to other children.

The poem 'Rocket Horse' can be used to fuel the children's imaginations. If they had a rocket horse, what would it look like? Where would they go – (reading the picture book listed in the books to read list: *Whatever Next* by Jill Murphy – may give them more ideas.)

> If I had a rocket horse
> I would zoom into space.
> I would travel past Mars,
> I would fly round the sun,
> and land on the moon.

The repetition of 'I would' in this poem helps children to see that a poem can have a pattern, and that this pattern will help to give it a rhythm. Ask the children to look out for poems that use repetition in this way.

Read the poem 'Only the Moon' by Wong May. Go through each idea with the children and check if they understand the imagery. Why does the new moon look like a cradle or a banana? Children might like to try something similar – 'When I was a baby I thought/ the stars were pinpricks in a black blanket. . .'

Look at the poems 'Star Travelling' by Andrew Collett and 'Riddle' by Sue Cowling. Both of these poems give clues as to what the poem is about. Using one of these poems as a model, children might like to try writing their own riddle poems for the moon, the sun, Mars, a spaceship, and so on.

After they have looked at 'What's that Shape?' by Gina Douthwaite, children may enjoy experimenting with simple shape poems of their own, perhaps for a full moon, a quarter moon, or one of the planets.

Julie Holder's poem 'The Alien' may prompt children to write their own descriptive poems. They could choose to write about either a funny alien or a scary one.

Encourage children to look for further examples of space poetry. These can be copied out and then illustrated. Build up a collection of poems and let children talk about their favourites. Let them practise reading and performing the poems adding actions and percussion accompaniment if appropriate.

Such activities as these will promote and reinforce the suggested work at various levels in the National Literacy Strategy.

About the Poets

Clare Bevan lives in Crowthorne, Berkshire with her husband, son and two cats. She was a teacher for many years and now writes stories and poems for children.

Barry Buckingham lives in Buckinghamshire. He was a head teacher for many years and has written numerous poems and stories for children.

John Coldwell was born in north London and now lives in Ramsgate. When he was a teenager his teacher wanted him to play rugby but he reckoned that writing poems was safer. He is now a teacher himself and encourages his pupils to avoid rugby by writing poems.

Andrew Collett spent his childhood in Newcastle-upon-Tyne but he now lives in Peterborough. He divides his time between writing and performing poetry. His work is featured in many anthologies.

Sue Cowling has lived in many different places but now lives in the Midlands. She writes children's poems about all sorts of things, including maths and science.

Gina Douthwaite lives high on the Yorkshire Wolds where she writes poetry and stories for children. She also runs *Poetry Parties* in schools and a collection of shape poetry, *Picture a Poem* was published by Hutchinson in 1994.

Julie Holder lives in London. She decided she wanted to be a writer after reading *The Water Babies* by Charles Kingsley. She started her writing career with a TV series for children called 'The Flumps'.

Tony Langham lives in Mytholmroyd, West Yorkshire. He teaches English to Pakistani and Bangladeshi children and they teach him how to do tricks with yo-yos.

Tony Mitton lived abroad for much of his early childhood. He read English at Cambridge University and then qualified as a teacher. He lives in Cambridge and his latest book of poetry for children is called *Plum* (Scholastic).

Brian Moses lives on the coast in Sussex. He writes and edits books for children and travels the country performing his poems.

Kjartan Poskitt lives in York. He worked for seven years with Keith Chegwin on the TV programmes *Swap Shop* and *Superstore* and has written a variety of books including *Murderous Maths* and *The Gobsmaking Galaxy* (Scholastic).

Christina Rosetti (1830-94) was an English poet who published a number of books of rhymes for young children including *Sing Song*, and *Goblin Market* – a fairy story in verse.

Marian Swinger lives beside the River Thames, not far from London. She enjoys writing poetry but makes her living as a photographer.

Clive Webster is a retired English teacher who lives in Worksop, Derbyshire. He has been writing verse – and worse – for over twenty years. He is a mad-keen sportsman.

Books to Read

The following books may be useful to use alongside the poems featured in this collection:

Whatever Next! by Jill Murphy (Macmillan Children's Books, 1995). Baby bear travels to the moon in his rocket box! A classic picture book.

The Monster Story-Teller by Jacqueline Wilson (Doubleday, 1997). A tiny monster whizzes Natalie off to his home planet in a mini flying saucer.

Noah and the Space Ark by Laura Cecil, illustrated by Emma Chichester Clark (Puffin Picture Book, 1998). It is some years into the future and a new Noah is building a rocket ship to take animals from Earth to a new world.

Spacebaby by Henrietta Branford (Collins, 1996). The Earth is losing weight. Gravity has gone wrong. It is now up to Spacebaby and his friends to see if they can save the Earth. A challenging read for confident readers in Year 2.

Aliens Stole My Underpants and other Intergalactic Poems compiled by Brian Moses (Macmillan, 1998). Fun poems about aliens in every shape and form!

Space Poems compiled by John Foster (Jackdaws, Oxford Reading Tree, 1991). More poems for this age range, from 'The Solar System Tour' to 'The Spaceship Race.'

Permissions
The compiler and publisher would like to thank the authors for allowing their poems to appear in this anthology. While every attempt has been made to gain permissions and provide an up-to-date biography, in some cases this has not been possible and we apologise for any omissions.

'What's that Shape' by Gina Douthwaite, from *Picture A Poem* appears by kind permission of Random House U.K. Ltd, Hutchinson, 1994; 'Three Cheers' from *Limericks* appears by permission of Henderson Publishing plc, 1996.

Index of First Lines